The 100 Most Powerful Prayers for Students

Toby Peterson

2

Copyright © 2017 PrayToTheWorld.com All Rights Reserved.

No part of this publication may be reproduced, distributed, or transmitted in any form or by any means, including photocopying, recording, or other electronic or mechanical methods, or by any information storage and retrieval system without the prior written permission of the publisher, except in the case of very brief quotations embodied in critical reviews and certain other noncommercial uses permitted by copyright law.

4

Do You Like Audiobooks?

The experience of having these read to you will, for many people, be more powerful than reading to yourself. For that reason, we are very happy to offer our readers the option to listen to our titles.

If you are not a member of Audible, you can actually get this for free just by signing up. In fact, you can cancel at anytime, and keep the book too.

Many of our readers have enjoyed this option. To learn more and get this audiobook for free, visit: PrayToTheWorld.com

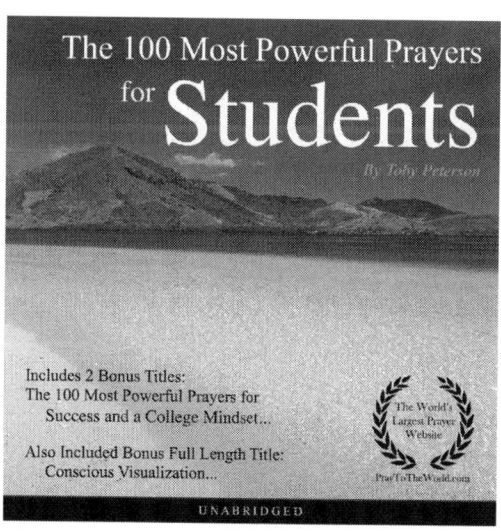

6

Want Free Books?
Or a Chance to Win a Kindle eReader?

From time to time we give away free copies of new releases. But promotions are very temporary. If you'd like to be notified when we're giving kindle books away for free, please consider signing up at the following:

PrayToTheWorld.com

Kindle readers are also given away as a draw periodically to subscribers...

*****

8

Table of Contents

Introduction..11
The 100 Most Powerful Prayers for Students..17

Bonus Titles:
The 100 Most Powerful Prayers for Success..41
The 100 Most Powerful Prayers for a College Mindset..65

Conclusion..89
Conscious Visualization..91
References..180

Introduction

In order to attain self-actualization and joy through God, you need to become the designer of your destiny, the author of your life story and the shipwright of your desired vessel. You will need to take responsibility for the success or failure of your life. We know the word responsibility can be somewhat frightening as it not only gives the impression that an enormous amount of work is required but it also speaks to the importance of this task. We agree that taking hold of your life is a significant step which requires a committed mindset. The process, however, this does not necessarily have to be a difficult or massive one. Every process consists of different stages; governing your destiny is certainly no different.

The key is to acknowledge the need to make the adjustments and then begin to make them. Initiating the transformation of your life and well being through prayer is easy. You can start by spending a few short minutes daily in reflection and prayer. Why not take that step of communicating with God, right now? You will be surprised at the powerful effect this simple action will have on your entire life changing process.

The knowledge that God gives you the capabilities to make these changes allows you to emancipate yourself from all fear and doubt. It, therefore, means you will need to first acknowledge that God will provide the mental emotional and spiritual resources needed and then believe in their abilities to accomplish what you need to. The reassurance that God has already given you what you need offers the comfort and security that you are indeed able to successfully make the changes in your life.

The process of regaining the joy, fulfillment, and happiness that God has for your life is effortless with this tried, tested and proven practice. Unlocking your true potential and achieve the goals, dreams, plans and aspirations that God meant for you to have lies with you. That's right, you already have the inherent ability, it simply needs to be accessed and used.

It has been used by the top performers of various groups in society from different industries; finance, education, and even sports. From the financial stalwarts, professors, scholars to Olympic champions, all have used this technique. During this year's Olympic games, it was interesting to find one consistent occurrence with many of the athletes and even more so with the champions. Prior to the signal from the starter for each major race, the competitors close their eyes and pray for a moment. What could they be praying about? Many of these sportsmen and women have won numerous medals and championships prior to the games. They are professionals… shouldn't they have this in the bag? They do, they simply are using the tried, proven and tested technique…

Before commencing they visualize, the event from start to finish with them executing what they have practiced and ultimately winning the said event. These vivid visions are a form of prayer, which has been used for many years. This is one example of how you can tap into the real power of prayer and how God is able to raise you up from the pitfalls any of life's challenges, which weigh you down.

Once you open up yourself to God's positive energy around, the process of creating the outcomes you desire becomes easier. After all, practice makes perfect.

Please do not misunderstand, Prayer isn't intended to make you into an ostrich where you stick your head in the sand and pretend that challenges or negative influences or impacts in your life are non-existent. Instead, prayer encourages you to increase your focus on the progressive end you want and the infinite support that God gives to help you make it happen. Prayer will not mandate that in a day you to get up from your seat and start a profitable multi-billion dollar business out of thin air. *However,* prayer will assist you to find your motivation, own it, and focus on it and in doing so drop all insecurities preventing you from accomplishing your goals. It, therefore, gives you the authority to confidently work with God toward the manifestation of your goals.

Many people lose their ability to focus on the positive energy, which God flows into the world. What with all the overwhelming pressures of daily activities and all the pressures and stresses associated with some, it is almost impossible to keep focus, right? Wrong. Your mindset and attitude will change as you integrate your positive building prayers in your daily routine. You will discover that the more your embrace the positive of any situation, the room for the anxiety and fear which act as stumbling blocks in the lives many people destroying their overall well-being becomes severely decreased.

The prayers here will ensure that you not only determine God's strength to continue your journey towards personal development in spite of the daily challenges and anxieties associated with them. God will release you from the cycle of pessimism and destructive mindset, which has been hindering you from accomplishing your goals for so long.

This book contains a number of prayers designed to help guide and motivate you as you continue on your spiritual journey of change. Any transformation begins in the spiritual realm. Your attitude and mindset determine your reaction to the daily struggles you will encounter. An optimistic attitude and mindset will seek to find the benefit or advantage of every situation; therefore, you will react with less anxiety and stress even when the situation becomes unbearable. These prayers are meant to assist you in maintaining your focus. Please feel free to integrate them into your daily routine. There is no reason to follow a particular routine with the prayers. This may mean you will utilize some while limiting the use of others. Remember the journey life is not unbending it is fluid. Figure out how, when, why and where they work for you. Finally, don't give up at the first attempt, remember everything is a process and practice makes perfect. You will see the difference God has made in your life in the just how your confidence level increases and how your apprehension decreases. The more this happens the closer you are to attaining your goals.

You can use these prayers *for any situation*. Once you start using them, you will find that specific prayers are brought to your consciousness whenever you find yourself in overwhelming situations. This is you learning to replace negative patterns in thinking and responding with prayer.

When you notice this happening more frequently, get excited, it means you are growing and the process is working. You are training your mind to work with God's natural flow of energy, which is always positive. We are created to operate as happy, healthy and fulfilled beings. Unfortunately, the complexities of the world have made it more difficult to find and maintain this sweet balance that God has fashioned with us. Damaging thoughts go against God's natural order and will unravel the people who harbor them. Through prayer, you will learn to remain consistent in absorbing and seeking out positive energies. These will transcend into all aspects of your life and influence the people around you. There is no reason to dwell on the loss, defeat, and regrets. It only takes the first few minutes of prayer…lost focus? Regroup and try again. Consider the following as your remedy for results.

1. Review the following list of prayers in full.
2. Pick five (5) to ten (10) prayers that powerfully resonate with you.
3. Repeat several times a day at different intervals. (Minimum five (5) times a day)
4. Use anything available to remind you even on a busy day: a daily planner, phone alarm, etc.
5. Do this consistently for ninety (90) days.

At the end of these ninety (90) days, you will notice, the occurrences in your life are aligned with your expressed desire and no longer just occur by default. You have the results, transfer to the next issue that you wish to change or overcome in your life.

Enjoy!

16

The 100 Most Powerful Prayers for Students

18

I am a great student and able to learn easily through God

I never worry about exams because I have confidence in my ability to learn.

Through The Lord's will, I see my studies as doors opening to the future.

I am able to study and to concentrate on what I have to learn.

Jesus, through you I have learned that concentrated effort gives endless rewards.

I will pass my exams because I am a capable student.

I am fortunate and will succeed in my life.

Thank you Lord for the ability to learn quickly and to adapt to change.

I am capable of standing tall, knowing my common sense will guide me through life.

I am a student of life and thrill in the joy of the lessons life gives me.

I am not afraid of learning new things.

I have the qualifications to be a student and to make the most of who I am.

God please guide me to understand that different people learn at different paces.

I can meditate on my successes and enjoy them to the fullest.

I am not afraid of failure because failure teaches me lessons that are positive.

I do not disappoint those around me, because I don't disappoint myself.

I see myself as a student of life and am always grateful for knowledge gained.

Thank The Lord for I am growing into a fully-fledged adult that I am able to love and care for.

I am happy in spirit because I am self-reliant.

I have eaten the food of life and have enjoyed my first tastes.

Because of God's will and grace, I will go forward in my life, taking the lessons I learn with me.

I pray that I will always be able to add to my knowledge by observing the world around me.

I feel that being a student is a privileged situation.

I am honored by the presence of people who teach.

I am not afraid of asking questions and it pays off.

God, I love learning and it helps me to grow as a person

I am not afraid of new lessons and embrace new ideas

I respect my teachers and they enhance my life

God, through you there is nothing too hard to learn.

I know that my life is filled with power when I listen to my teachers

I have the inner resources to succeed as a student

I am capable and very happy in my life as a student as I have Christ by my side

I have planned out a path for my life and will succeed

I love my student life and live it to its fullest every day for Jesus.

I enjoy the company of my fellow students

I am able to study and save plenty of time for fun and worship with other Christians

I study well because I am an active listener

I love the idea that my knowledge base is expanding

I enjoy being a student of life and learning more about God

I am proud of my achievements as a student.

I have plenty of confidence to get me through college.

I will always have room in my life for learning as I have learned all of God's teachings

I know that everything I learn will be put to good use.

I never question the merits of learning as I never question The Lord

I am able to produce good quality work to be proud of

I love that I am able to gain great grades

I know my family and Jesus are proud of my achievements

I am a student of life as well as a student in the classroom

I am going through this phase of life and loving every moment of it, thank you for the opportunities God

I am able to listen and learn easily

I respect my teachers and the lessons that they impart as I respect God's teachings

I am a grade A student and proud of it

I increase my level of understanding life through my studies

I never see learning as negative as Jesus has taught me so much as well.

My teachers like me and this is reflected in my learning ability

I am able to achieve great things in my life by learning.

I am setting a solid path in my life through my understanding and worshipping of Jesus

I am a brilliant student and stay that way because I am focused

I meditate and this keeps me grounded

I believe in being the best human being I can be so God can look down on me like a proud Father

I know that my teachers enhance my knowledge

I am learning independence in a positive environment

I am thankful to God I am becoming an adult and understand the responsibility attached to life.

I will always make my parents proud of my achievements

I never waste learning time because it helps me to grow as a human.

Jesus, please guide me to love the work that I do and thrive on challenges.

I am a team player and respect my fellow students as The Lord watches over me

I am never jealous of others because jealousy makes people less important

I have everything I need to succeed as I have The Lord.

I can walk proudly into a classroom knowing I will learn something new.

I embrace new experiences.

Thank you for your grace God, I am good at expressing myself in words.

I can surprise myself each day by learning more about life.

I always go for the best grades and never give half-heartedly.

I give my best to my studies and know it's enough.

I have great friends and supporters and I am loved by The Father of the Son.

I enjoy sports and feel they let me expend excess energy

I love competition and thrive on trying to do my best.

Due to my relationship with Jesus Christ, I am able to see with clarity my progress in college.

I know my own weaknesses and work toward strengthening them.

I take a pride in having great handwriting.

I am able to use computers fluently

I love to lose myself in a great book that teaches me

God, please help me to be proud of my ability to exceed my own expectations

I do the best I can and best is always good enough.

I am able to share growing up with my fellow roommates

I love the company of others the same age as I am.

I enjoy the challenge of getting my test work ready on time.

Lord, please help me to never be late with my homework.

I always do more than I am asked to

I excel in learning because I know it helps me to assure my future.

I love waking to another day of learning.

I have no complexes about who I am as God has made me this way.

I am confident in my ability to ask the right questions

I always finish my homework before partying

I enjoy partying as much as I enjoy being up to date with my studies

I am able to lose myself in music when I need to relax

Lord, please help me to be able to trust myself to get great results.

I am top in everything I put my heart into because this is God's plan for me.

I make great competition for my fellow students.

40

The 100 Most Powerful Prayers for Success

42

God, thank you for making me a magnet for success and good fortune.

Lord, I am grateful for the knowledge you have provided me.

I am considered a major success through the Lord's grace.

Heavenly Father, I humbly ask you to make me more successful every day in every way.

Lovingly God, through your will, I live a positive life and only attract the best into my life.

My Lord, please guide me in thinking only of success.

*With my Creator's guidance, I have learned from the past,
I live in the present and plan for the better future.*

*I see success in everything I do, O Lord, with small
successes building large success.*

*Dear God, I trust in you my good fortune and my good life
as the result of my success.*

*Through the Lord's grace, I am consistently presented with
new opportunities.*

Thank you, my Father, for a world filled with love, abundance, happiness and success.

Heavenly God, please guide me in making SUCCESS mandatory.

I believe and trust in you, my God, with my own eventual success.

My Lord, please help me in overcoming my fears to move in the direction of my goals.

God's blessings make me worthy and deserving of everything that I want in my life.

Through your will, Lord, I am building a successful company every day.

Dear God, thank you for making me create daily opportunities for the growth of myself and others.

Heavenly Father, I am grateful that I am earning more every day by doing something I love.

O Lord, I humbly ask you to bless me with limitless opportunities.

Dear God, please energize me by the challenges I meet in my business.

Through Lord's will and guidance, I am growing in success.

Please help me, O God, to open my heart to receive rich opportunities.

Heavenly Father, please guide me in becoming more prosperous, everyday, in every way.

To my Creator, I am grateful for receiving avalanches of money every month.

Dear God, please help me in attracting successful people.

I am becoming more successful every day through God's will.

O God, please help me in taking the right steps towards my goal.

I am very proud of my achievements, Lord, and I owe these to you.

Because of you, my Lord, I am inspired and have the power to accomplish everything I need today.

I am happy, successful and fulfilled through God's grace.

Heavenly God, I thank you, because at every turn, opportunity appears before me.

I am becoming better at what I do everyday with my Lord's assistance.

Thank you, O Lord, for letting me enjoy being optimistic.

Lovingly Father, I am grateful that my wealth is increasing more and more everyday.

Dear Lord, please provide me more guidance in being passionate about increasing my fortune.

My God, thank you for providing me confidence that reigns in any business setting.

O Lord, I humbly ask you to make me a success magnet.

I have created the perfect business for myself through God's grace.

Heavenly Father, thank you for letting me receive money through my hard work.

Dear Lord, please bless me with courage and perseverance to succeed.

O God, I am grateful that you help me in focusing on my many achievements.

My Lord, please guide me in achieving great and successful results.

I choose happiness and success with God's grace.

Through my Creator's will, I live to succeed.

I am successful because I help others to succeed with my Lord's assistance.

Dear Father, please help me to believe in myself and in my ability to succeed.

Heavenly Father, make me open to new opportunities and success.

Lovingly Father, please bless me with a successful career that I deserve.

O Lord, please provide me the right persistence until I succeed.

Dear God, please let me trust in my abilities.

Heavenly God, please make all of my thoughts, plans and ideas lead me straight to success.

I humbly ask you to make opportunities and advantages come with each door that I open, my God.

Thank you for making me an example of success and triumph, my Dear Father.

God is creating the perfect life for myself, my family, and my peer group.

My Lord, please make me enjoy getting out of my comfort zone and strive for what's best.

The Creator makes me aglow with enthusiasm as I work towardsnew goals.

Dear God, please let me make every certain success is followed with fulfillment.

Thank you for letting me celebrate my continuing good fortune, my Lord.

Please let me demonstrate the excellence within me, My Father.

Dear God, please let me focus on what is truly essential.

Heavenly Father, I humbly ask you to let me move forward eagerly.

O Lord, thank you for letting me live a life that is an exciting adventure, filled with opportunity and reward.

Please make me committed to my goals, Dear Lord.

Father, please let me be persistent in all that I do.

Lord, please help me in creating money-making ideas for my business.

Please guide me in acting more like a successful person, O God.

Dear God, please let me be open and receptive to new avenues of income.

Thank you for letting me ensure prosperity of others, O Lord, for I know there is more than enough for everyone.

Heavenly Father, I open my heart to receive this day, rich with opportunities.

I have made being successful my natural state of being through God's will.

The Lord made me a solution-oriented individual; all problems are solvable.

God, thank you for making all my actions aimed at reaching my goal. I achieve my goals one after the other with your guidance.

Please make me utilize all ethical channels to become successful, O Father, for I leave no stone unturned to find success.

I always spot opportunities and utilize them. New doors are always opening for me through God's will.

Dear God, You are in charge of my life. When I make a decision, please make that decision eventually lead to success.

I am in charge of my emotions, desires and abilities, but I focus only on success through God's assistance.

I realize that success is a result of right thinking and hard work. I excel in both because of my Lord's guidance.

Dear Father, thank you for always making me prepared. Hence, luck always favors me.

Heavenly God, thank you for making me realize that success is an ongoing process. After one success, I focus on another.

Thank you for making me free of negative thinking, O Lord. I embrace only positive thoughts.

Dear Lord, please put success in everything I do. Small successes build up into large success for me.

I am a person of action and a person of vision through God's grace. Naturally, success is the only outcome of whatever I do.

The Creator blessed me with success as my birth-right and I will achieve it. Thought, determination and action eventually result in success.

Lord, thank you for making me inspired, enthusiastic and success bound. My journey ends only after achieving success.

Dear God, I deserve to be successful. My good fortune and my good life is the result of my success.

I can't do everything today, but I can take one small step through God's grace.

Help me do what no one else is willing to do, O Lord, for I aim to be successful.

Almighty Father, please make me believe in my ability to manifest my dreams.

I attract success in all areas of my life through God's will.

Thank you for making me always think positively and achieve great things, my Lord.

Dear Father, please bless me with the will and the drive to succeed.

I am blessed with a life that is full of abundance & success from the Creator.

Lord, thank you for transforming me into someone who always succeeds.

Heavenly God, please make me believe deeply in my ability to attract success.

Thank you for blessing me with success, achievement, and abundance that easily flows into my life, O Lord.

I always seem to find a way to succeed, one way or another through God's will.

Dear God, thank you for making me motivated and productive.

I know others see me as someone who persistently strives for success; that is all because of your guidance, my Lord.

Thank you for always making me successful in every aspect of my life, lovingly Father.

Almighty Father, thank you for not letting tardiness prevail, for I get what I want for my business.

64

The 100 Most Powerful Prayers for a College Mindset

Through the grace of God, I am smart enough to study college.

I will take advantage of my youth by studying while I'm young and able.

Jesus, because of you, I will not waste my college life.

I will not regret my decisions when I'm older.

I will learn as much as I can while I have the time.

I pray to maximize the resources available to me.

I will not look back at my college years thinking I made big mistakes.

I will make sure to get the education I need to prepare me for real life.

I will set my priorities straight with God by my side

I will choose my commitments wisely.

I will not disappoint my parents and family.

I will be able to provide for my family in the future if I study well.

I will make a schedule to allocate my time properly.

Jesus, please guide me to challenge myself in every class that I will take.

Jesus, please help me to be energetic.

I have chosen a course that leads to my desired career path.

I can pass all my exams and graduate on time.

I will choose my classes wisely, through great faith.

I will also take classes that interest me.

I pray to be an active participant in my classes.

I am studying to get a meaningful degree.

I study enough for all my classes, with Jesus.

I am attracted to knowledge and knowledge is attracted to me.

I make good decisions in my college life with the aid of God.

I always manage my time wisely.

I can do everything that I set out to do.

I will take care of myself while striving to pass my classes.

I will not let go of myself, through the Lord's holiness.

I will not give up, with God by my side.

I am admired for my knowledge.

I live in good terms with my dorm mates/roommates/peers.

I can get along well with other people in my class.

I prepare myself in tests through Jesus.

Thank you God, I can handle any obstacles.

I have a good memory and I can pass my tests.

I think critically, with the aid of our Lord.

I can analyze things better than most people.

I will not let college change the way I look at other people.

I can handle any stress college life brings me.

I am happy to be a college student.

Jesus, because of you, I improve my study habits constantly.

I am making a dream a reality by going to college.

As a Christian, I enjoy learning.

I am in complete control of my studies.

I use the knowledge I gain to help others.

I am grateful for the opportunity to study college.

Thank you God almighty, I get better at studying each day.

I am able to get along with my professors.

Thank you God almighty, I can learn things easily.

I think college is one of the most exciting parts of my life.

I talk about my college experience with my family because it's important to me.

I am at my best when I'm studying.

By God's grace, I can overcome any problem that comes to me.

I maintain a positive outlook to help me with my everyday life.

I go to classes every day because I enjoy doing so.

I love studying in my college!

I have school pride because I love studying here.

Because of God's, guidance, I love answering exams.

I absorb useful information like a sponge.

As a Christian, I try to learn everything I can during my short time here.

I believe there are no wasted time as long as I'm studying.

I believe there are no wasted classes as long as I'm enjoying what I'm learning.

I can achieve the high standards that I set for myself, with the Lord by my side.

As a child of Christ, I will not mold myself to the expectations of other people.

I don't have the responsibility to please everyone.

I think my education will make me more of myself.

Through the Lord's holiness, I study and learn at my own pace.

I believe education can help me to become a better person.

Thank you God, I will always be thankful for this chance to study.

I promise to use this chance to its full potential.

I can do anything if I will focus on it.

Through Jesus, I will set aside my fears.

Through Christ, I will achieve my goals.

Jesus, because of you, I am a great student.

I make meaningful contributions to my classes.

I value myself and my abilities.

I deserve the good grades I receive.

I sleep knowing I tried my best and if I fail, it's not my fault.

I like to help others learn things as easily as me.

As a Christian, I will remain humble and kind despite my college education.

As a child of Christ, I will not look down on other people just because I was able to study.

I will see each and every one of my colleagues as a unique individual.

I will use my education to improve the future of society, with God by my side.

I promise that I will share the benefits of my college education to other people.

Thank you Jesus, I am smart and creative enough to succeed.

With the guidance of our Lord, I will focus on doing my assignments.

I will read and write as much as possible.

With God almighty, I choose to be positive.

By God's grace, I will not let the pressures of society bring me down.

I will rise up: study, learn, and graduate!

I will make sure to have fun while in college.

I will choose my college friends wisely.

I will not be swayed by the negative opinions of my peers.

Through the Lord's holiness, I will achieve!

I am the best at what I do!

I can pass with flying colors.

I will not compare myself to my classmates.

I believe that everything that is happening is happening for a reason.

I am brave enough to face my exams!

With Jesus by my side, I will graduate and I will face the world with confidence

Thank You!

I want to sincerely thank you for reading this book!

Let me finish though by saying the work isn't done here. These must be put to use repetitively, and on a daily basis to see changes in your life.

Remember to follow the ninety-day plan outlined in the introduction to maximize your results.

Can I ask you for a very quick favor? Can you leave a review on our Amazon.com detail page to tell us about your progress and how you enjoyed the book?

It's really easy, and you can do it right here:

    amazon.com/review/create-review

We take the time to go over each review personally, and your feedback in invaluable to us as writers, and others that wish to see the same change in their lives as you:)

Thank You!

Copyright 2016 WorldAffirmations.com - All rights reserved.

This document is geared towards providing exact and reliable information in regards to the topic and issue covered. The publication is sold with the idea that the publisher is not required to render accounting, officially permitted, or otherwise, qualified services. If advice is necessary, legal or professional, a practiced individual in the profession should be ordered.

- From a Declaration of Principles which was accepted and approved equally by a Committee of the American Bar Association and a Committee of Publishers and Associations.

In no way is it legal to reproduce, duplicate, or transmit any part of this document in either electronic means or in printed format. Recording of this publication is strictly prohibited and any storage of this document is not allowed unless with written permission from the publisher. All rights reserved.

The information provided herein is stated to be truthful and consistent, in that any liability, in terms of inattention or otherwise, by any usage or abuse of any policies, processes, or directions contained within is the solitary and utter responsibility of the recipient reader. Under no circumstances will any legal responsibility or blame be held against the publisher for any reparation, damages, or monetary loss due to the information herein, either directly or indirectly.

Respective authors own all copyrights not held by the publisher.

The information herein is offered for informational purposes solely, and is universal as so. The presentation of the information is without contract or any type of guarantee assurance.

The trademarks that are used are without any consent, and the publication of the trademark is without permission or backing by the trademark owner. All trademarks and brands within this book are for clarifying purposes only and are the owned by the owners themselves, not affiliated with this document.

Table of Contents

Foreword

Introduction

Chapter 1 – Step 1 – Setting Your Goals

Chapter 2 – Step 2 – Daily Visualization of Your Goals

Chapter 3 – Step 3 – Relaxing in Stressful Situations

Chapter 4 – Step 4 – Boost Your Self-Confidence

Chapter 5 – Step 5 – Overcoming Obstacles

Chapter 6 – The Taking Action Visualization

Conclusion

References

Foreword

Until recent times, mostly sports psychologists and personal trainers that were teaching athletes to visualize success valued visualization. After much studying and application, however, it has been found that the power of conscious visualization can help people from all walks of life reach their goals.

Do some research yourself. You will find athletes, movie actors, entrepreneurs, and people from all areas and occupations that have learned the incredible power of visualization and how it can help them succeed in achieving their wildest dreams. Conscious visualization propels you past the obstacles that you may face and helps you reach the biggest goals that you set for yourself.

Now, get out there and be the best version of you that you can be. This book is going to teach you all of the visualization techniques that you need so that you soar over your obstacles and achieve even the most challenging of goals that you set for yourself.

I want to wish you luck and success as you start, continue on, and complete your journey.

Toby Peterson

100

Introduction

Oprah Winfrey, Will Smith, and Arnold Schwarzenegger are just three of many well-known celebrities that have attributed at least some of their success to the power of conscious visualization. There are stories from celebrities around the world that prove one thing; visualization can be the driving factor in your success.

It is no surprise that these and many other successful individuals rely on visualization to power them forward. Stop for a moment and think about the last time you were faced with an intimidating situation, whether it was a presentation at work or meeting your future in-laws for the first time. How did you feel beforehand? What thoughts were running through your head?

If you are like most people who have not yet learned the power of conscious visualization, then you were probably worried about the situation you were faced with. You may have even made yourself panic over the situation, by worrying about what could go wrong instead of what could go right.

The key to conscious visualization is that it helps you overcome obstacles. When you can visualize the end result, you can power yourself through any of the roadblocks in your way and give yourself a confidence in yourself that you did not even know you had.

The good news is that while many successful people attribute their success to conscious visualization, you can do it too. You do not have to be wealthy or extraordinarily talented to make your splash in the world and reach your goals. The only thing that you need is the power of your own mind and the steps included in this book.

As you read, you will find that your results may improve by listening to the visualizations instead of just reading them. If this is the case, you can purchase the audio version of this book.

In this book, you will find five separate steps that will propel you to your own success. You will also find a bonus chapter, which addresses affirmations that you can use to further the success of conscious visualization and boost your confidence in yourself. Once you have reached the end of this book, you will have learned a regimen that will propel you forward to reach your greatest dreams. You will be able to overcome obstacles, feel confident in yourself, and so much more. All you have to do is visualize- read on to find out how.

Chapter 1 - Step 1 - Setting Your Goals

The first step of conscious visualization is knowing what your goals are. In order for visualization to propel you to success, you must be able to pinpoint the things that you want in life. From there, you must be able to choose a realistic and directed visualization that is going to help you reach success. This chapter will teach you all about setting goals and the techniques that you can use to keep them in the forefront of your mind.

How to Properly Set Goals

Be Realistic and Have a Plan for Follow Through

Consider for a moment that your goal is to be rich one day. You start every morning by visualizing yourself sitting in a bathtub of money. How likely do you think it is that this will work?

The truth is that whether or not the visualization works depends on your course of action following the visualization. Imagine one scenario where the person visualizing wealth does not have a job. They live at their parent's house, do not put in job applications or make wise investments, and do nothing to better themselves. Even with a great visualization, it is very unlikely that this person is going to reach their goals.

Imagine a second scenario. This person also dreams of great riches and their visions are perfect down to the satisfaction. When they go to spend money on something they don't need, they may think of this vision. Instead of spending the money, they invest it in a savings account that accrues interest and increases their wealth over time. This person accompanied their visualizations with the right actions.

As you are setting your goal, it is important to have a plan of action as well. You can visualize success all you want, but it will not work if you are intentionally sabotaging yourself or hiding in your parent's basement all day. You have to have the follow through of the right actions in order to reach your goals.

Be Specific

One of the keys to successful visualization is being specific. In order for your visualizations to be successful, you must make your goals as successful as possible. For example, do not imagine yourself becoming wealthy. Instead, imagine yourself being wealthy by doing well in the stock market, opening the business you always dreamed of, being promoted in your place of work, or cashing in on wise investments one day.

Break Your Goal Into Steps

If you have a long-term goal, you will find that it is helpful to break it up into steps. Every goal that you have is a process, especially in the long-term. You will not just rise to the top in your company from a lower level position. Instead, you will go through a series of promotions until you are at the top. As you are planning each goal, take a moment to break it down into a series of steps. If you want a car, for example, you may set goals to save a certain amount of money back each month until you can afford it.

Write Your Major Goals Down on Note Cards

If you have several goals, then you may find it beneficial to write each individual goal down on note cards. On the front, you can write down a summary of the goal. On the back, break your goal down into steps. You may also find it helpful to write down helpful affirmations that pertain to that specific goal or your specific visualization that you use to picture the goal. If applicable, you can also write down the timeframe in which you want to complete each step of the goal.

Chapter 2 - Step 2 - Daily Visualization of Your Goals

In order for visualization to be successful, it is important to make it part of a daily regimen. During this regimen, you will be visualizing success of all of your objectives for the day and tie them back to your larger goals. As you are reading about the regimen in the conclusion of this book, you should refer back to this chapter for instructions.

The Science of Conscious Visualization

When you carry out an activity or a thought, a certain set of neurons lights up, as well as the neural pathways between them. Conscious visualization works because visualizing a certain scenario lights up the neural pathways that tell the brain to perform that action, whatever it may be. Every time that you carry out this activity, the neural pathways strengthen and the mind will eventually be able to carry out the task instantaneously. Visualizing certain scenarios frequently, therefore, strengthens the neural pathways and makes these behaviors easier. This means you will be more likely to perform well when you are actually doing the activity or behavior.

For more evidence and information on the way that visualization works, check out the references section at the end of the book.

Planning Your Objectives

As you will learn later in this book, there is more than one type of conscious visualization that can help you on the road to success. For this type of visualization, you will want to start by planning out your objectives for the day. Make a physical list of the things that you want to accomplish. These can be tasks like making time for yourself or working on housework or they can be behavioral changes like being more confident or interacting more with your coworkers.

Visualizing Your Objectives

Go to a quiet area where you can be comfortable and relax. Sit or lie down and relax in silence for a few moments. Then, read over your list of objectives to get them fresh in your mind. Visualize yourself going through your day and completing each of these objectives. Feel yourself confidently tacking each item on your list and physical sensations that you may experience. Give yourself confidence that you will be able to complete each of your goals by envisioning each of them.

As you visualize, you may find it helpful to observe yourself in first person. As you go through your vision, pay close attention the way everything feels. Imagine yourself from the inside of your body and that you are interacting with people and your surroundings.

Visualizing Your Success

Imagine yourself basking for a moment after each small success, thinking about how the task accomplished a goal (a clean house can reduce stress) or how it will help propel you forward in life. Visualize yourself completing all of your goals and how it will feel when you are rewarding yourself at the end of the day.

Example of Daily Conscious Visualization

For the purpose of this exercise, imagine that you have a note card with the following goals written down on it:

1. To reach out to your coworkers by inviting someone to have lunch with you
2. To make it to the gym after work
3. To start your research for a presentation at work
4. To spend at least an hour not working and having 'me' time before bed

Sit or lie down in your quiet space. Close your eyes and take a few deep breaths to relax. Then, read the goals that you have written on the note card to bring them to the forefront of your mind. Alternatively, you can visualize each goal separately and read the objectives on the note card one at a time.

Start by visualizing yourself walking through the doors to your job. Feel your confidence as you walk toward one of your coworkers and ask them to lunch. Visualize them accepting your invitation. Then, imagine conversing with them over lunch, being as specific as you can. Imagine the happiness that you will feel at the chance to make a new friend and the sense of companionship that you feel from interacting with others.

Then, visualize yourself leaving from work and feeling energized. You eat a small snack and drive (or walk) to the gym. You have a satisfying workout. When you finish, imagine the sense of accomplishment and pride that you feel for doing something for yourself and working toward your weight loss goals.

Next, imagine yourself driving to your house. You cook and eat dinner. Once you are finished, you walk to the computer and begin your research for work. Visualize the keyboard beneath your fingers as you take notes. After you are satisfied with the work that you have done, visualize yourself pausing to bask in your sense of accomplishment. Enjoy the relief that you feel with the project now being started.

Finally, imagine what you are going to do before bedtime. Now that you are satisfied with your work for the night, you do not go straight to bed and watch television or play on your phone until you pass out. Think about what you want to do for yourself, whether you want to read a book, take a hot bath, do yoga, color, or do another activity. Imagine the activity from start to finish and then feel the sense of pride that fills you after completing all of your objectives for the day. Focus on this feeling until it gives you a warm, glowing feeling of happiness and success.

Chapter 3 - Step 3 - Learning to Relax in Stressful Situations

While this book is about creating a regular regimen for success, you will find there are times where conscious visualization can help you relax to handle a stressful situation better. Some situations where this technique may be applicable include before a job interview, test, presentation at school or work, a first date, meeting your spouse's parents, or talking to someone in an uncomfortable situation. Visualization can often be used for these types of encounters on a per-case basis to help you come out successful on the other side.

Identifying Your Challenge Situations

In order to know when visualization can benefit you throughout the day, you must be able to identify which situations call for a little extra help. Some people, for example, fear public speaking and may struggle any time that they must speak to a group. Others may find that their most challenging situations include encounters with others.

A good way to identify which situations stress you is to pay attention to physical cues and your thought patterns. Some physical cues that you may experience in a stressful situation include excessive sweating, clammy palms, and a rapid heartbeat. Some common thought patterns include self-defeating thoughts like "I can't do this," "I'm going to do terrible," and "I'm not good enough," as well as worries about what may go wrong in the situation.

If you find yourself struggling to notice specific patterns, consider keeping a journal. Make note of any of the times that you feel overly stressed or notice the thoughts and feelings from the previous paragraph. Write down the time of day, what was happening at the time, and which thoughts or physical sensations you experienced. You should also make note of who was around at the time, what you were thinking about, and any other relevant information. If you keep good notes, you will eventually be able to go over them and recognize the various patterns. Once you see the patterns, you will be able to plan for stressful situations before they even occur.

Visualization for Challenging Situations

Go To a Quiet Room

Before you tackle the challenging situation, put yourself in a calm, quiet environment where you can focus. If you are at home, this could be your bedroom, your garden, or another area you have set up. If you are at work, a good place to relax could be an empty conference room or your office. Sit or lie down and close your eyes. Pay close attention to your breathing and bring yourself into a state of relaxation.

Picture Your Success

Once you are relaxed, picture your success overcoming the obstacle from the second that you walk through the door. Be as detailed as you can and visualize yourself overcoming every obstacle that comes in your way. Here is an example of a visualization that you could use if you were giving a presentation at work:

You are standing outside of the office door, knowing that you are about to walk in and give a presentation to a room full of people. You are dressed nicely, well groomed, and feeling confident. You turn the doorknob and walk confidently across the room to the front with your head held high. Your presentation is already set up, including any visuals or power point material that you may have. You casually introduce yourself to the group and give a brief summary of what is about to be discussed. Then, you pull note cards out of your pocket and begin to give your presentation, only glancing at the note cards to keep you on track. Your voice is calm and sure.

At the end of the presentation, some of your audience has questions. You are well prepared and feel confident as you are answering their questions. At the end of the presentation, you feel pleased and know that the committee values your idea.

Take a Few Breaths and Succeed

After you have done your visualization, you are ready to tackle your challenge. Take a few deep breaths, imagine the feeling of success once again, and excel in the stressful situation.

Chapter 4 - Step 4 - Using Visualization to Boost Your Self-Confidence

One of the reasons that visualization works is because it increases your self-confidence. Think about the last time you faced a situation that you worried about. Did you panic yourself into thinking all of the bad things that could happen? What was the result of the situation? If you did fret over what could go wrong instead of what could go right, it is likely that you set yourself up for failure. After all, how can you be confident about the outcome of a situation when you have so many doubts about it in the first place? In this chapter, you will learn how to use visualization to boost your self-confidence so that you stop doubting yourself in challenging situations.

#1: Identify Why You Are Lacking Self-Confidence

Before you can go about changing your lack of self-confidence, you must understand the reasons that you act and think the way that you do. Below are some of the most common reasons that people lack self-confidence.

You Talk Negatively to Yourself

Have you ever heard the expression, "I am my own self critic."? While being a critic of yourself can help you find your flaws to improve them, it is not helpful if you are holding yourself back with your criticisms. For example, people who talk negatively to themselves often set themselves up for failure before they are even faced with a situation. They may have to give a presentation at work and talk down to themselves beforehand, saying things like "I am not good enough," "They will not like my idea," or "Why should I even bother?" The problem with this is that talking negatively to yourself makes you think that you will fail. If you believe that you are going to fail, it is much more likely that you will have a bad outcome.

You Are Afraid to Take Risks

Some people just find themselves more outgoing than others. Some people believe that this is a personality difference that is ingrained from birth, while others blame it on a child's upbringing. Regardless, if you find that you are afraid of taking risks, it becomes more likely that you will lack self-confidence. The reason for this is that you probably had fewer experiences because you are more likely to say "no" to trying new things. This lack of experience can result in a lack of self-confidence.

You Do Not Know How to Be Confident

Have you ever found yourself looking at a friend or coworker and wondering how they are able to be so confident? It seems that some people are born confident, while others struggle even to interact with other people on a day-to-day basis. If you find yourself feeling as if confidence is something that you are born with and that you did not get the gene, remember that it is a learned skill. Anyone can be confident in his or her abilities- it just takes the right self-talk and visualizations to encourage you on your way.

#2: Know How Confident People Act

The first step in uncovering your own confidence is knowing how confident people act. Make a list of behaviors of confident people. For example, to you, confidence may mean talking to people more, making your ideas known, being able to showcase your talents, or not being afraid to bring up difficult subjects. Think about the way that confident people walk, how they interact with others, and how they make their ideas known. If you do not know, spend some time watching some of the most confident people you know.

#3: Change Your Thoughts and Behaviours

Once you know how confident people behave, you can start to act that way. You will find that everything you do can exude confidence if you do it properly. The way you walk, talk, and interact with others can have profound effects on the level of confidence that you feel. Once you know how confident people act, start to follow in their footsteps to develop your own self-confidence.

If you find yourself struggling with negative thinking that is costing you your self-confidence, it can be important to change the way that you think. Start by recognizing your negative thought patterns (I am worthless, I cannot do this, I will mess this up) and changing them by stating the opposite. Build yourself up instead of tearing yourself down and you will find that the result is greater confidence.

#4: Visualize Yourself Confidently Handling Your Challenges

Once you are ready to make the commitment to self-confidence, use visualization to see yourself feeling confident in everything that you do. When you are doing your daily visualizations, feel the way that your shoulders and back stretch out when you stand tall and envision yourself speaking clearly and loudly. Imagine the warmth that feels your chest when you are confident enough in your ideas that you can freely share them with others and the friendships that may result from being more outgoing and communicating with others. Clearly visualize yourself tackling each challenge and then feel the satisfaction when you do so.

Example of Visualization for Self-Confidence

In this scenario, you have been gabbing with a coworker for several weeks. You decide to ask him/her out on a date but you are incredibly nervous. Before you talk to your coworker, you would perform this visualization.

The morning before, you carefully pick out one of your favorite outfits that is attractive and comfortable. You remember to put on deodorant and brush your teeth and your clothes are nice. When you get to the office, you visualize yourself entering the door with your head up and your shoulders back, exuding an air of confidence. You walk to the water cooler and take a deep breath. Your words come out clear, "Will you go to lunch with me?" Visualize that your coworker has said yes and imagine the sense of excitement and content that you will feel once you have asked.

Chapter 5 - Step 5 - Overcoming Obstacles

Conscious visualization is all about visualizing success and only thinking of the positive things that will happen in your life, right? Well, yes and no. Positive visualization can help propel you to success. However, you do have to realize that not everything that happens in life is in your control. Additionally, it is natural for you to face obstacles or have things come up that challenge your goals and your motivation toward them, as well as your peace of mind. This chapter will teach you about the techniques that you can use to overcome your obstacles so that they do not get in the way of your positive visualization.

Let Go of Things That Are Out of Your Control

It would be very unnatural for someone to go through life without any types of struggle. Even if you use visualization to fill your life with as much positivity, self-confidence, and success that you can muster, things are going to arise that may set you back. For example, you may have fitness goals but then have a relative you were close to pass away. There may be a few days where you struggle to make it to the gym. In this case, it is best to remember that you cannot control what has happened. Allow yourself time to grieve and forgive yourself if you skip the gym for a few days. What matters is that you will get back on track, regardless of the setbacks you experience.

Visualization Example for Releasing Negative Thoughts

For this exercise, go to a quiet area where you can relax. Sit or lie in a comfortable position and start to breathe. As you breathe, focus your mind on all of your worries and negative thoughts. Allow yourself to dwell for one breath cycle. Then, inhale a deep breath through your nose, filling your stomach and chest until you cannot any longer. Imagine that this breath is all of the negativity inside of you. Exhale it in a slow but strong woosh, breathing out through your mouth.

Repeat this visualization a few times. Then, start to breathe in more slowly and deliberately. Visualize that positive vibes and feelings are filling you with each inward breath. If you find yourself dwelling on any more negative thoughts, exhale them out. Do this until nothing but positivity exists inside of you.

Look At Negative Encounters As a Lesson

Negative experiences and people are a part of life, as are the ways that we let them affect us. When you are faced with negative experiences, look at them as a lesson. Imagine for a moment that you have a friend who betrayed your trust. Rather than seeing it as a negative experience, consider the friendship for what it was worth. Maybe the situation happened so that they betrayed your trust with this and not something even more serious.

Prepare for the Worst Case Scenario

Sometimes, regardless of how much we prepare, we find ourselves struggling to find the positivity and confidence to deal with a situation. Additionally, there are situations that we may have a negative outcome from, even with positive visualization. If you find yourself worrying about an obstacle that has arisen or at a loss for how to handle an issue, think about the worst thing that could happen. Often, people who chronically worry exaggerate the real dangers of a situation. Once you think about the worst thing that could happen, consider the likelihood of the even happening.

If you do find that it is likely the scenario could happen, consider what you could do in the situation. If there is nothing that you can do, then sit back and try to relax until you hear something new. It is not helpful to worry over situations that you have no control over.

Make a Plan to Tackle the Obstacle

When you are handling a real obstacle that you must deal with, the least stressful and most helpful thing that you can do to work toward your own success is make a plan to tackle the obstacle and get it out of your way.

Developing an End Goal

The first step of any plan is to know exactly what you intend to do. The reason for this is having a clear objective will keep you on track as you work toward the end goal. Consider exactly what the obstacle is that you are facing and what it would mean to overcome it. Then, write the obstacle down at the top of a piece of paper to keep you on track as you come up with a plan to tackle the obstacle.

Writing the Plan

Once you have an end goal, you can start breaking it down into steps. Each step of the plan should be manageable on its own and work toward the major goal of overcoming your obstacle. In addition to breaking down the steps, you may want to consider when each step should be done or write down specifics about how you intend to do each step (when steps are necessary).

Consciously Visualizing the Course of Action

After you have a clear-cut plan, you can begin visualization. Once again, you will go to a quiet environment and sit or lay comfortable. Close your eyes and focus on your breaths. Once you are relaxed, read over the individual steps of your plan, as well as your end goal. After you have read the steps, close your eyes once again. Visualize yourself completing each individual step and then envision the satisfaction that goes along with it. Feel the pride that accompanies you after completing each step and then the sense of happiness that will follow when you complete your entire goal.

Example Visualization for Overcoming Obstacles

For this visualization, imagine that you are at work one day and a new person starts. It turns out to be someone from high school that you do not get along with. You remember the incident and want to clear the air with your coworker but are shy. The pressure increases when your boss assigns you to work together.

The goal in this situation would be to address the misunderstanding between yourself and your classmate in the past, agree to leave the disagreement in the past, and work toward success at the office. To do this, you will need to come up with a plan of action to speak to your coworker.

Visualize yourself walking toward your coworker, with your shoulders back, your back straight, and your head held high. Feel the confidence that is oozing from you and filling the air. As you approach your coworker, you think about what you want to say once again. You remind your coworker of this misunderstanding and assure him or her that you want to leave the past in the past. Then, you inform them that you have been assigned to work together recently and you would like to use that time to let bygones be bygones and work toward the success of the team. Seal your conversation with a friendly handshake and a plan to meet up in the future to discuss the project.

After visualizing the conversation, imagine yourself walking away. Feel the confidence and reassurance that now fills you, instead of the worry that was present earlier.

Chapter 6 – The Taking Action Visualization

Sometimes, the perfect companion to your visualization exercises is affirmations. Self-affirmations are short statements that give you the confidence and self-esteem that you need to start taking action in your life. After all, your visualizations will not be nearly as helpful if you do not have the follow through to go with them.

In this chapter, you will find 100 affirmations that will give you the confidence and the power necessary to start taking action in your life. Thee will have a much greater impact if you read them out loud or listen to them audibly:

Every action that I take moves me one step closer to my goals…

Each action that I take toward my goal moves me closer to success…

I strive to accelerate my progress toward my goals every day…

Each of my actions moves me toward bigger and better successes…

Every one of my actions creates positive opportunities and experiences…

I act on each opportunity that is presented to me…

I am motivated toward my goals and my overall success…

Every one of my actions reflects the person that I dream of becoming…

I know what needs to be done and act on what needs to be done immediately…

Every step that I take will be in a positive direction forward toward my goals…

I am inspired each day to take actions toward my progress…

I see success as a journey and work to move on to bigger and better things every day…

My actions and attitude are able to propel me toward success…

All of my energy is directed toward positive actions…

I push myself to complete more difficult tasks first so that the rest of the day flows easily…

My actions demonstrate my commitment toward progress and success…

I invest my emotions, actions, and energies into producing positive results…

I am in control of my successes by making positive changes every day…

I look for new ways to pursue my goals every day…

My commitment to my goals can be seen through my behaviors…

I honor each of my intentions by acting on them every day…

I write down all of the actions I must take to strive toward my goals…

My list of goals is ongoing and I strive toward it daily…

I feel a sense of invigoration with each positive action that I take…

My visualizations make me feel empowered to succeed with each of my goals…

I keep myself on track with moving toward my goals…

I know the first step in any goals is taking action…

I know that action is both required and necessary to meet my goals…

I feel confident in my ability to change my own life with visualization…

I know that changes must be made to strive for bigger and better things…

I know that taking action is much more important than just talking about goals...

I feel great satisfaction each time I cross something off of my goals list...

I visualize myself being incredibly productive in working toward my goals today...

I only put my energy toward actions that are empowering and encouraging...

I work toward my dreams relentlessly...

I know that I can take charge of my life and work toward my dreams…

Every action that I take toward my goals is deliberate and intentional…

I talk and think less and take action toward my goals more…

Every positive action that I take throughout the day will bring me closer to my dreams…

The thoughts that I think and the actions that I take create the reality that I live in…

I use positive thoughts and positive actions to move me toward my goals…

I find that the words I speak and the actions I take reflect positive moves forward…

It brings me joy to see the progress I take toward my goals each day…

I embrace success and refuse to believe any negative thoughts that will hold me back…

I sever attachment from people and things holding me back from my success…

I do have choices and I am free to create my own reality and my highest level of success…

I let go of negative things and make more room for success to come into my life…

I release the need to compare to others and realize that my own success should reflect my needs…

I judge my own success by my own wants and desires and not the wants and desires of others…

I will show the world what I can offer and fulfill my true purpose…

I am here to leave a positive imprint on the world and will take the actions to do so…

I release the negativity from my life so that I can focus on positive actions…

I commit to being a positive influence on myself and the world around me…

I am thankful for each day and the actions that I will take to push myself toward success…

My options are not limited in any situations and I do have the power to make choices…

My wants and desires deserve to be fulfilled because I deserve it…

Today holds infinite possibilities in the number of ways it can be a positive influence on my life…

I will interact with people that will help me on my path to greatness…

Instead of worrying about not having enough time, I will focus on using the time that I do have to work toward my goals…

My main focus will be serving my life's purpose and I will view anything that does not benefit me as a distraction…

I feel confident that once I commit to my dreams, they will start coming true…

I find it easy to direct my thoughts and actions so that they reflect my goals…

I will stay away from drama and negativity and surround myself with people and circumstances that bring positivity and success to my life…

I know that negative circumstances are a part of life and that I am confident to continue pursuing my dreams after a setback…

I choose to forgive others so that I can move forward with my life…

A wrong turn does not mean starting over, it just means following a new route…

I have the confidence and power to know that I can reach my goals…

I have great trust in my ability to make decisions to help me reach my goals…

I commit to doing at least one thing each day to progress toward my dreams…

I will view my journey of progress as what has already been accomplished, instead of focusing on what still needs to be completed…

My dreams and visions shape what I should accomplish, not the desires of others…

I know that I am meant to do big things and refuse to let anyone hold me back…

I choose to be who I want to be and accept others as who they are and know that we are all on our own paths…

My approval of myself is more important than seeking approval from others…

Some situations are out of my control and I refuse to worry about what I cannot control…

I do not need anyone to make me successful, I am in charge of my own success…

The decisions I make affect my success and I do not need the approval of others…

I choose to be the best version of myself that I can be…

I refuse to let others affect me reaching my goals…

I will be mindful and aware as I go throughout the day…

I will be aware of the ways that my actions influence my success throughout the day...

Fear will not get in the way of me striving for the things that I want...

The path to happiness starts with me and I am ready to commit to that change...

My visualizations will give me the courage to act in a way that will push me to achieve my goals...

I know what I deserve from life and I take responsibility for making it happen...

I refuse to give others the power to make me angry because I am responsible for the way I react and feel…

I am committed to my vision and use my visualizations to drive me forward…

Even the smallest of actions steps push me toward my goal…

Focusing my intentions and actions will bring me closer to my goal…

I will stay on my course, regardless of any obstacles I may face…

I know that some things happen to be a lesson and I can still persevere after setbacks…

I will always let in clear opportunities…

I have a passion to find my purpose and this will drive me toward my dreams…

I have endless talents and I will start using them today…

The qualities needed to reach my goals are inside of me…

I will abandon old habits that hold me back in place of new ones…

I will use visualization any time I find myself being discouraged…

I can handle any of the challenges that life may throw my way…

My visualizations will become my future…

Obstacles are moving out of my way and I am heading toward greatness…

You should read these affirmations out loud to yourself or listen to a recording of them. Once you have a clearer, more directed picture of your goals, you can write out your own affirmations to reflect on.

Conclusion

It is highly recommended that you continue to use visualization as you come across obstacles in life or as you find yourself reaching for new goals. You can change the visualizations that you use for any goal that you set - so continue to strive for bigger and better things once you have reached your current goals. There is no limit to the things that you can accomplish when you are able to visualize your success.

The next logical step here is to practice conscious visualization and start changing your life. Follow a regimen of practicing visualization for 15 minutes every morning before you start your day and every night before you go to bed. Use the steps provided in this book for your visualization. Follow this regimen for a period of at least 90 days and watch how it propels you forward and pushes you to succeed in every area of your life.

Best of luck as you push forward and change your life!

Jason.

References

Brouziyne, M., & Molinaro, C. (2005). Mental imagery combined with physical practice of approach shots for golf beginners. Perceptual and motor skills., 101(1), 203-11. Retrieved from
http://www.ncbi.nlm.nih.gov/pubmed/16350625

Canfield, J. (2014, April 1). Visualize and affirm your desired outcomes: A step-by-step guide - America's leading authority on creating success and personal fulfillment. Retrieved September 25, 2016, from Success & Goal Achievement, http://jackcanfield.com/visualize-and-affirm-your-desired-outcomes-a-step-by-step-guide/

Hudson, P. (2016, June 15). The power of visualization in manifesting your success. Retrieved September 25, 2016, from Entrepreneurship,
http://elitedaily.com/money/entrepreneurship/the-power-of-visualization-in-manifesting-your-success/

Mueller, S. (2016, August 2). The power of creative visualization. Retrieved September 25, 2016, from Mind,
http://www.planetofsuccess.com/blog/2016/power-of-creative-visualization/

Niles, F. (2011, June 17). Why goal visualization works. Huffington Post. Retrieved from http://www.huffingtonpost.com/frank-niles-phd/visualization-goals_b_878424.html

Reyes, A. (2012, April 4). Alejandro Reyes. Retrieved September 25, 2016, from http://expertenough.com/1898/visualization-works

Made in the USA
Lexington, KY
27 November 2018